ADELE

The Girl With The Golden Voice

This paperback edition published in 2016
First published in hardback in 2014

Copyright © Wayland 2014

Wayland, an imprint of
Hachette Children's Group
Part of Hodder & Stoughton
Carmelite House
50 Victoria Embankment
London EC4Y 0DZ

Senior editor: Julia Adams
Produced for Wayland by Dynamo
Written by Hettie Bingham

Picture acknowledgements:
Key: b=bottom, t=top, r=right, l=left, m=middle, bgd=background

Alamy P7 tr, p8 br, p15 b, p25 m Alamy Celebrity/Alamy; **Corbis** P1 m, p16 b
Lucy Nicholson/Reuters; p21 mr Pool Reuters; **Getty** P11 b Getty Images; p5
b, p27 bl Mark Davis/WireImage; p2 tr, p13 b Redferns; p19 m, p30 tr Wire
Image; **iStock** p5 tr Tomas_Mina, p6 tr Bunwit; **REX** P22 mr Richard Young/
REX; **Shutterstock** Backgrounds and Doodles: PILart, JelenaA, Julijamilaja,
Bazzier, art_of_sun, VectorShots, Boobl, S.Edel. p7 ml wongstock, p8 tl kak2s,
p8 m Stephen Rees, p9 br Cidonia, p14 bl aimy27feb, p16 m Buslik, p18 b
Harijs A, p18 m Nicemonkey, p20 t Nicholas 852; **Splash** P4 m, p29 br Jen
Lowery/Splash News.

Dewey classification: 782.4'2164'092-dc23
ISBN 978 0 7502 8965 8
Library e-book ISBN 978 0 7502 8560 5

Printed in China
10 9 8 7 6 5 4 3 2 1

Wayland is a division of Hachette Children's Books,
an Hachette UK company.
www.hachette.co.uk

ADELE

ADELE

The Girl With The Golden Voice

■ Singer, songwriter and Oscar-winner; Adele is an international music sensation. She is known across the globe, but she still has her feet planted firmly on the ground.

'I LOVE ENTERTAINING PEOPLE. IT'S A HUGE DEAL THAT PEOPLE PAY THEIR HARD-EARNED MONEY, NO MATTER HOW MUCH OR HOW LITTLE, TO SPEND AN HOUR OF THEIR DAY TO COME AND WATCH ME. I DON'T TAKE THAT RESPONSIBILITY LIGHTLY.'

NAME: Adele Laurie Blue Adkins

BORN: 5 May 1988

HOMETOWN: West Norwood, South London, England

HEIGHT: 1.75 metres (5 ft 9 inches)

HONOURS: MBE

PARTNER: Simon Konecki

SON: Angelo James Konecki (born 19 October 2012)

SCHOOL: The BRIT School for Performing Arts and Technology

LIKES: Meeting her friends for lunch, false eyelashes, hairpieces, going out with no makeup on so she's not recognized, and cracking jokes

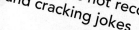

Adele
as a kid

*I*n May 1988, Adele was born to a teenage mother, Penny Adkins, whom Adele has described as:

'HONEST AND OPEN AND SO SUPPORTIVE.'

At just 18 years old, Penny did not have a lot of money, but she worked hard to make ends meet. Living in a flat in Tottenham, North London, she worked as a furniture-maker, masseuse and also organized activities for adults with special needs. Adele's father, Mark Evans, left when she was three and so Penny raised her as a single parent.

*W*hen Adele was a little girl she had a red toy guitar that her mother had bought her from a charity shop. Adele loved to strum it and soon began to sing along. She was a super-star in the making.

*W*hile Penny worked, Adele was often cared for by two of her aunts, Anita and Kim. 'Mum's side [of the family] is massive. All brilliant. Dominated by women and all really helping each other out, so even though she brought me up on her own, it was kind of a team effort,' Adele has said.

*G*et this!
Adele performed at an early age. As a 5-year-old, her mum allowed her to stand on the table at dinner parties and belt out *Dreams* by Gabrielle.

When she was 9, Adele and her mother moved to Brighton in West Sussex. They stayed there for two years before moving to South London when Adele was 11 years old. They lived first in Brixton before settling in West Norwood, where they lived in a flat above a discount store.

'IT ALL COMES FROM IMPERSONATING THE SPICE GIRLS AND GABRIELLE. I DID LITTLE CONCERTS IN MY ROOM FOR MY MUM AND HER FRIENDS. MY MUM'S QUITE ARTY - SHE'D GET ALL THESE LAMPS AND SHINE THEM UP TO MAKE ONE BIG SPOTLIGHT. THEY'D ALL SIT ON THE BED.'

Adele started her secondary education at Chestnut Grove School in Balham, South West London. The friends she made there introduced her to R&B music, which she loved. Adele has spoken of the fun she had sitting in the playground and singing with her friends during her time there. When she was 14, she moved to the BRIT School for Performing Arts and Technology where she began to learn about the music business.

BRIT School

When Adele was accepted into the BRIT School for Performing Arts at the age of 14, it was the first step on her way to fame.

'AS SOON AS I GOT A MICROPHONE IN MY HAND, WHEN I WAS ABOUT 14, I REALIZED I WANTED TO DO THIS.'

The BRIT School describes itself as being 'unique and pioneering' in its approach to education. It is a state-funded city college for 14–19-year-olds who want training in the performing arts, media, art and design, and the technologies that make performance possible. It is not a typical stage school and receives a lot of support from the music industry.

Adele clearly enjoyed her time there.

'IT HAD FREE REHEARSAL ROOMS AND FREE EQUIPMENT AND I WAS LISTENING TO MUSIC ALL DAY, EVERY DAY FOR YEARS. THE MUSIC COURSE WAS REALLY WICKED. THERE WAS NO DANCING OR ANYTHING LIKE THAT. NO JAZZ HANDS.'

When Adele was in her second year at BRIT School, Shingai Shoniwa, the Noisettes singer (who was yet to make it big in the music business), moved in next door to her. Adele used to go round to her flat to sing with her. The experience cemented Adele's desire to write songs and she became focused on her music studies.

'SHE (SHINGAI) IS AN AMAZING SINGER. I USED TO HEAR HER THROUGH THE WALLS. I'D GO ROUND AND WE'D JAM AND STUFF LIKE THAT.'

'IT WAS CLEAR SHE (Adele) WAS GOING TO BE A STAR. SOME PEOPLE WERE THAT STEP ABOVE EVERYONE ELSE. AND ADELE WAS ONE OF THEM.'

Allan Rose, former schoolmate at BRIT School

Adele continued to pursue her ambitions and soon became an accomplished songwriter. She performed her song *Daydreamer* on an acoustic guitar to her fellow students at the BRIT School. Liz Penney, Adele's music teacher at the time, remembers the performance. 'In our feedback session afterwards everyone spoke about how they were really wowed by her performance. It was something special,' she said. The song later went on to be the first track on her album *19*.

Get this!

Jessie J, Leona Lewis and Amy Winehouse all used to be BRIT School pupils as well. Jessie J was in the same year as Adele and sometimes used to hang out with her at lunchtime.

'YOU COULD HEAR HER (Adele) LAUGH FROM A MILE DOWN THE CORRIDOR.'

Jessie J

When Adele posted some songs she had recorded for a school project on Myspace, her rich, soulful voiced began to attract attention.

It was one of Adele's friends who had the idea of setting up a Myspace page for her. It turned out to be a good idea; Adele's songs soon got noticed.

In December 2006, her friend Jack Peñate, also a singer and songwriter, asked her to be his support act at the Troubadour, a club in Earls Court, London. It was a small venue, with room for about 100 people in the audience. Adele went on stage alone with a guitar and began to sing.

'THE WHOLE ROOM WAS PACKED… IT WAS HOT. IT WAS DISGUSTING… THE WHOLE ROOM WAS SILENT, AND I SAW THESE RANDOM GIRLS JUST, LIKE, CRYING.'

Get this!

In 2007, Adele's friend, the singer Jamie T, released her song Hometown Glory as a single on his own label, Pacemaker Records, as a 7" vinyl single. Only 500 copies were pressed and the song didn't make it into the charts. Later the song became a massive hit (see page 12).

Adele found the experience so amazing that she decided she couldn't live without it. She once said:

'THERE'S NOTHING MORE FREEING THAN PLAYING LIVE, NOTHING.'

Out

ick Huggett, an A&R man at XL Recordings at that time, heard Adele and was impressed. He contacted her through her Myspace page and Adele went to meet him. When Nick realized that Adele didn't have a manager, he had a word with his friend, Jonathan Dickins, who runs September Management.

'I'D NEVER HEARD OF XL... I TOOK ONE OF MY FRIENDS WITH ME [TO THE FIRST MEETING] BECAUSE I THOUGHT MAYBE IT WAS SOME WEIRDO ON THE INTERNET.'

'HE (Nick Hugget) SAID I SHOULD CHECK THIS GIRL OUT,'

Jonathan explained.

'WE HAD ONE MEETING AND JUST GOT ON GREAT. SHE WAS 18, JUST OUT OF COLLEGE, AND WANTED TO MAKE A CAREER IN MUSIC.'

'MOST PEOPLE DON'T LIKE THE WAY THEIR VOICE SOUNDS WHEN IT'S RECORDED. I WAS JUST SO EXCITED BY THE WHOLE THING THAT I WASN'T BOTHERED WHAT IT SOUNDED LIKE.'

(ADELE, ON HER FIRST EXPERIENCES OF RECORDING)

Early SUCCESS

Adele started working with Jonathan at September Management and, before long, she had signed a record contract with XL Recordings and begun writing and recording her own songs.

Taking inspiration from her experience of breaking up with a boyfriend, the songs Adele wrote were very personal to her; she found she could be more open about her feelings through her songs than she could be in day-to-day life.

Towards the end of 2007, Adele began appearing on TV shows in the UK including *Friday Night with Jonathan Ross, Richard & Judy* and *Lily Allen and Friends*. Adele's unique sound was catching on with the public; she won the BBC's 'Sound of 2008' poll and her fans eagerly awaited more of her music.

Named after the age she was when she wrote most of the songs on it, Adele's first album was called *19*. It was released in January 2008 along with the single, *Chasing Pavements*. It entered the UK album charts at number 1, with *Chasing Pavements* reaching number 2 in the singles charts. Her previous single, *Hometown Glory*, received renewed interest and entered the charts at number 32 due to downloads, giving her two top 40 hits at the same time.

♡ *Get this!*
An Evening with Adele was a world tour which began in May 2008 and ended in June 2009.

During a short American tour in March 2008 XL Recordings agreed a joint venture with Columbia Records to release *19* in the US in June of the same year.

Adele did not gain the instant success in America that she had done in the UK. But that all changed in October 2008 when Adele appeared on the American show *Saturday Night Live*. She performed her singles *Chasing Pavements* and *Cold Shoulder* and, the next day, *19* went to the top of the iTunes charts due to all the downloads she had received as a result of her appearance. The American public had finally embraced her talent. Adele's fourth single from *19* was *Make You Feel My Love*, which reached number 4 in the UK charts.

'HEARTBREAK CAN DEFINITELY GIVE YOU A DEEPER SENSIBILITY FOR WRITING SONGS. I DREW ON A LOT OF HEARTBREAK WHEN I WAS WRITING MY FIRST ALBUM. I DIDN'T MEAN TO BUT I JUST DID.'

INFLUENCES

Adele grew up with many musical influences, some from the music her mother listened to and some from the chart music she enjoyed with her school friends.

Pop music was a big part of Adele's childhood.

'I LISTENED TO JEFF BUCKLEY AND JOAN ARMATRADING BECAUSE OF MY MUM, BUT E17 WERE MY BOY BAND, AND I LOVED BACKSTREET BOYS, AQUA, DESTINY'S CHILD, MISSY ELLIOTT.'

She is still a huge fan of the Spice Girls, Britney Spears, Scissor Sisters, MIKA and Katy Perry.

Adele is also a massive fan of Beyoncé.

'SHE'S BEEN A HUGE AND CONSTANT PART OF MY LIFE AS AN ARTIST SINCE I WAS ABOUT 10 OR 11. I LOVE HOW ALL OF HER SONGS ARE ABOUT EMPOWERMENT… I THINK SHE'S REALLY INSPIRING. SHE'S BEAUTIFUL. SHE'S RIDICULOUSLY TALENTED, AND SHE IS ONE OF THE KINDEST PEOPLE I'VE EVER MET.'

When Adele was 14, she bought two jazz CDs from a bargain bin; it changed her perspective completely. It was the style of the jazz singers on the covers that caught her eye at first – she wanted to copy it.

'I REMEMBER BEING OUT AT THE RECORD STORE HMV WITH ALL MY FRIENDS… THEY HAD A TWO-FOR-ONE DEAL, TWO CDS FOR A FIVER, AND I BOUGHT ELLA FITZGERALD AND ETTA JAMES. I BOUGHT THEM BECAUSE I LOVED THEIR IMMACULATE HAIRDOS AND ETTA JAMES'S EYES – THE ORIGINAL AMY WINEHOUSE EYES! I LOVED THE VINTAGE LOOK OF IT,' she said.

The CDs sat gathering dust in her bedroom for a while until Adele decided to listen to them. And when she did, she said,

'IT CHANGED MY LIFE... IT WAS SO HEARTFELT COMPARED WITH THE MUSIC I'D BEEN LISTENING TO.'

Discovering jazz changed Adele's taste in music and she began to explore other genres, too.

'I TAUGHT MYSELF HOW TO SING BY LISTENING TO ELLA FITZGERALD FOR ACROBATICS AND SCALES, ETTA JAMES FOR PASSION AND ROBERTA FLACK FOR CONTROL.'

'I KIND OF GOT INTO THE OLD LEGENDS – ROBERTA FLACK, JOHNNY CASH, DIANA ROSS AND THE SUPREMES.'

'CHART MUSIC WAS ALL I EVER KNEW. SO WHEN I LISTENED TO THE ETTAS AND THE ELLAS, IT SOUNDS SO CHEESY, BUT IT WAS LIKE AN AWAKENING. I WAS LIKE, OH, RIGHT, SOME PEOPLE HAVE PROPER LONGEVITY AND ARE LEGENDS. I WAS SO INSPIRED THAT AS A 15-YEAR-OLD I WAS LISTENING TO MUSIC THAT HAD BEEN MADE IN THE 40s.'

GLOBAL FAME

Already established as an international artist, Adele's popularity continued to climb. The release of her second album secured her a top place in the music industry.

Again named after her age at the time of recording, Adele's eagerly awaited second album, 21, was released in January 2011. Once more the songs were inspired by the breakup of a relationship with a boyfriend, featuring feelings of anger, heartbreak, and forgiveness. The album was a massive hit, selling over 26 million copies worldwide by 2013.

Get this!
When 21 was released, Adele's first album, 19, started selling more copies and came back into the UK album charts.

Rolling in the Deep was the first single to be released from 21. Adele put her many musical influences to good use to produce a massive hit which she described at the time as a 'dark bluesy gospel disco tune'. The single was a number 1 hit in 11 countries, and her first in America. It went on to sell over 14 million copies and spent 65 weeks in the US charts.

When Someone Like You, Adele's second single from 21, was released, it reached number 1 in the UK charts after Adele performed it at the BRIT Awards. The tracks Set Fire to the Rain, Rumour Has It and Turning Tables were all released as singles during 2011.

Adele Live was the concert tour that took place during 2011 to promote 21. Adele toured Europe and America with a five-piece band and backing singers, although some of her songs were performed with just a piano. During the tour, Adele suffered from problems with her throat and had to cancel some of the concerts. She eventually needed surgery after she suffered a haemorrhage that caused bleeding near her vocal chords. As a result the tour ended earlier than planned. Luckily, Adele went on to make a full recovery.

'I'M REALLY FRUSTRATED. I WAS HOPING WITH A WEEK'S REST I'D BE BETTER TO SING AGAIN STRAIGHT AWAY. HOWEVER THERE IS ABSOLUTELY NOTHING I CAN DO BUT TAKE THE DOCTOR'S ADVICE AND REST SOME MORE. I'M SO SORRY. SEE YOU SOON, LOVE ADELE.'

ADELE'S STATEMENT AFTER CANCELLING NINE TOUR DATES IN AMERICA

SKYFALL

After months of rumours, Adele confirmed in October 2012 that she had co-written and performed the theme song for the James Bond movie *Skyfall*.

*A*dele composed the song with Paul Epworth, who had previously co-written Rolling in the Deep with her. Adele said that she had felt 'a little hesitant at first to be involved with the theme song for *Skyfall*' because of the instant spotlight and pressure that always comes with writing a Bond song – especially one which was to be released on the 50th anniversary of Dr. No, the first ever James Bond movie. When she met the James Bond film producer, Sam Mendes, she even told him that she wasn't the right person for the job explaining:

'MY SONGS ARE PERSONAL, I WRITE FROM THE HEART.'

He told her to:

'JUST WRITE A PERSONAL SONG'.

Adele left the meeting with a script tucked under her arm and, once she had read it, realized it was something that sh

Get this!

Adele let slip that she was working on the theme song during an interview on Jonathan Ross's chat show in 2011, saying: 'I'm going back in the studio in November, fingers crossed... well this is actually a theme, what I've got to do for, um... Wow. That's really giving something away isn't it?'

Adele had never written a song to order before. All her previous songs had been inspired by events in her own life. She later said that she had enjoyed the experience, finding it 'a lot of fun'.

Skyfall was recorded at Abbey Road studios in London with a 77-piece orchestra. 'When we recorded the strings, it was one of the proudest moments of my life,' Adele said.

'I'LL BE BACKCOMBING MY HAIR WHEN I'M 60 TELLING PEOPLE I WAS A BOND GIRL BACK IN THE DAY, I'M SURE.'

Skyfall was the first Bond theme to win an Academy Award for Best Original Song – one of many awards the song won (see page 21).

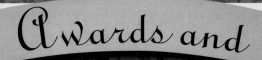

Awards and

Adele has been winning awards
since early on in her career and it wasn't long
before she was breaking records too. The
awards and honours have continued to come thick
and fast, making her one of the top artists of the 21st century.

Adele hit the ground running in 2009 when she won two Grammy Awards for Best New Artist and Best Female Pop Vocal Performance. Adele dedicated the awards to her mother and London.

At the 2012 Grammy Awards Adele scooped up six awards, winning every category that she had been nominated in. She won Song of the Year for *Rolling in the Deep*, Best Pop Solo Performance for *Someone Like You*, Best Pop Vocal Album and Album of the Year for *21*, and Record of the Year and Best Short Form Music Video for *Rolling In the Deep*.

'I JUST WANT TO SAY, MUM... YOUR GIRL DID GOOD!'

Adele at the Grammy Awards, 2012

Get this!

In 2009, the British Prime Minister Gordon Brown sent Adele a thank-you letter for her music, telling her that: 'WITH THE TROUBLES THAT THE COUNTRY'S IN FINANCIALLY, YOU'RE A LIGHT AT THE END OF THE TUNNEL'.

Adele was named as Songwriter of the Year at the Ivor Novello Awards in 2012. At the same ceremony, her song *Rolling in the Deep* won Most Performed Work of 2011. It also won a BMI Award for being the most played song on American TV and radio in 2011.

In 2012, Adele became the first woman in America's Billboard Hot 100's history to have three songs in the top 10 at the same time by a solo artist. Her album 21 also broke the record for the longest-running number 1 album by a woman in Billboard history.

Adele's Bond theme, *Skyfall*, won a raft of awards, starting with an Academy Award for Best Original Song in 2013. This was soon followed by a Golden Globe Award, again for Best Original Song. A Critics' Choice Award came next for Best Song. The same year it also won a BRIT Award for Best British Single and then went on to win a Grammy in 2014 for Best Song Written for Visual Media.

In the Queen's 2013 Birthday Honours, Adele was appointed MBE (Member of the Most Excellent Order of the British Empire) for services to music. She collected her MBE at Buckingham Palace from Prince Charles.

'IT WAS AN HONOUR TO BE RECOGNIZED AND A VERY PROUD MOMENT TO BE AWARDED ALONGSIDE SUCH WONDERFUL AND INSPIRATIONAL PEOPLE. VERY POSH INDEED.'

ADELE ON RECEIVING HER MBE

Family Life

It is clear that Adele has always had a very close relationship with her mother, Penny Adkins, and greatly admires her. Adele even has a 'one penny' tattoo on her wrist as a tribute to her. Now Adele is a working mother herself, with all the challenges that brings.

Adele always speaks warmly of her mother and often mentions her when accepting awards.

'SHE'S THE CALMEST PERSON, REALLY STRONG AND CLEVER AND BEAUTIFUL.'

Adele once said.

'SHE HAD ME REALLY YOUNG. AND THERE WAS LOADS OF STUFF SHE WANTED TO DO THAT SHE DIDN'T GET TO, SO SHE'S MAKING SURE SHE'S DOING IT NOW.'

When Adele became successful, she was able to make her mother's life a little easier, and gave her a flat in London's Notting Hill.

Adele now lives near Brighton in West Sussex with her partner, Simon Konecki.

Get this!

Adele puts her loud voice down to having a big extended family with lots of aunts and cousins. She once explained.

'YOU HAD TO FIGHT TO GET YOUR VOICE HEARD BECAUSE EVERYONE WAS SCREAMING AND CHATTING AT THE SAME TIME.'

Because Adele has always written very personal songs, the public know that her private life hasn't always run smoothly. When she met Simon Konecki, however, things took a turn for the better. Adele and Simon first appeared in public as a couple at the 2012 Grammy Awards. In June that year Adele had some exciting news to share:

'I'M DELIGHTED TO ANNOUNCE THAT SIMON AND I ARE EXPECTING OUR FIRST CHILD TOGETHER. I WANTED YOU TO HEAR THE NEWS DIRECT FROM ME, OBVIOUSLY WE'RE OVER THE MOON AND VERY EXCITED, BUT PLEASE RESPECT OUR PRIVACY AT THIS PRECIOUS TIME. YOURS ALWAYS, ADELE XX.'

'WHEN IT COMES TO STAYING MYSELF – MY CAREER ISN'T MY LIFE, IT DOESN'T COME HOME WITH ME.'

Simon is CEO of British charity Drop4Drop. He left a career in banking because he felt it unfair that 1.2 billion people – more than one sixth of world's population, do not have access to clean water. His charity aims to provide safe, clean water for all. Adele went on Twitter to urge her fans to support the charity. Simon has a daughter from a previous marriage.

On 19 October 2012, Adele and Simon became the proud parents of Angelo James Konecki. Four months later, Adele commented on motherhood while at the Grammy awards saying:

'I'VE BEEN UP SINCE 6 AM, SO I'M QUITE TIRED, BUT IT'S NICE.'

ADELE IN PUBLIC and private

We know a lot of personal things about Adele through the words of her songs, which are often about her relationships, but she tries to keep much of her life out of the spotlight.

During her first world tour in 2008, Adele cancelled dates saying that she had some 'family issues'. She later explained that she had been having problems with a boyfriend and had been drinking too much alcohol:

'WE REFER TO THAT PERIOD AS MY E.L.C. MY EARLY LIFE CRISIS. NOW I'M SOBER, I'M LIKE, I CAN'T BELIEVE I DID THAT – IT SEEMS SO UNGRATEFUL.'

On stage, Adele's emotions often spill out and she has talked in detail about the meaning of the songs to her audiences. Her personal feelings are bound together with her work. But although Adele has not been shy about sharing her feelings, she has kept the identities of the ex-boyfriends she sings about very private.

Adele tries to make sure she takes time out for herself. 'I have to take time and live a little bit. There were a good two years between my first and second albums, so it'll be the same this time,' she said when asked about her third album. She likes to live a normal life with her family and old friends, who are all as close to her as ever.

Adele once explained:

'OF COURSE I'M BOWLED OVER BY PEOPLE'S RESPONSE TO 21, AND WHEN I MEET ARTISTS I LOVE, IT BLOWS MY MIND. BUT IT BAFFLES ME AS WELL. I GO HOME AND MY BEST FRIEND LAUGHS AT ME, RATHER THAN GOING TO A CELEBRITY-STUDDED PARTY TO RUB SHOULDERS WITH PEOPLE WHO KNOW ME BUT WHO I DON'T KNOW.'

'I HAVE TO HAVE THE CONFIDENCE TO LET PEOPLE THAT I DON'T KNOW LISTEN TO MY MUSIC, BECAUSE IT'S SO PERSONAL.'
'I DO GIVE AS GOOD AS I GET... I KNOW I PLAY THE VICTIM, BUT... THAT POOR BOY; HE'S A VILLAIN THESE DAYS!'
'EVERYONE KNOWS WHAT IT'S LIKE TO LOSE SOMEONE THAT YOU LOVE IN SOME SHAPE OR FORM... WHICH IS OBVIOUSLY WHY SO MANY PEOPLE LIKE THIS SONG [SOMEONE LIKE YOU].'

Charity work

Adele has always found time in her busy schedule to show her support for various different causes by giving performances, donating items and collecting for charity.

In 2008, Adele performed at two concerts for Keep a Child Alive, a charity that offers care and support to children and families affected by HIV.

Adele performed at the Brooklyn Academy of Music in New York in 2009 for the American cable network company VH1's Save The Music Foundation. This is an organization dedicated to restoring music education in American schools.

Adele gave a free concert at the nightclub, Heaven, in 2011 for Pride London, the organizers of London's annual Gay Pride Parade.

The charity MusiCares, founded by the Grammys to support musicians in need, has also benefited from Adele's work. She performed at a benefit gig in Los Angeles in 2009 and donated autographed items for charity auctions in 2011 and 2012.

During her tour in 2011, Adele asked all backstage guests to donate a minimum of $20 to the UK charity Sands – an organization that supports people affected by the death of a baby. Adele collected $13,000 for the charity.

Adele is a supporter of Drop4Drop, the charity that her partner, Simon, runs. After encouraging her fans to support the charity, the Daydreamer/Drop4Drop alliance was formed in 2012 by a group of Adele's fans. The Official Adele Daydreamers started out as a small group of people across the world who wanted to put their common interest – Adele – to good use. Just three months after forming the alliance they reached their goal of raising enough money to build 21 water wells for people in desperate need of clean drinking water. The wells will supply more than 25,000 people with water for life.

'THE CASH HAS STARTED TRICKLING IN, BUT I DON'T COME FROM ANY MONEY SO I HELP PEOPLE. I GIVE MONEY TO CHARITY AND TO FRIENDS AND FAMILY.'

How well do you know...

ADELE

By now you should know lots of things about Adele. Test your knowledge of her by answering these questions:

1 In which area of London was Adele born?

a) Croydon
b) Clapham
c) Tottenham

2 What colour was Adele's toy guitar?

a) Pink
b) Red
c) Silver

3 What is the title of Adele's first single?

a) Someone Like You
b) Hometown Glory
c) Skyfall

4 What was the name of the school that Adele attended from the age of 14?

a) BRIT School
b) Fame Academy
c) Norwood Comprehensive

5 What is Adele's mother's name?

a) Gabriella
b) Jenny
c) Penny

6 Which famous singer went to school with Adele?

a) Rihanna
b) Jessie J
c) Beyoncé

7 What is the name of the record company Adele is signed to?

a) Virgin
b) XL Recordings
c) Polygram

8 What was the title of Adele's second album?

a) 21
b) 19
c) 23

9 In which year was Adele born?

a) 1990
b) 1979
c) 1988

10 Which Gabrielle song did Adele sing to her mother's friends when she was five years old?

a) Fallen Angel
b) I Wish
c) Dreams

ANSWERS

1	c) Tottenham
2	b) Red
3	b) *Hometown Glory*
4	a) BRIT School
5	c) Penny
6	b) Jessie J
7	b) XL Recordings
8	a) *21*
9	c) 1988
10	c) *Dreams*

You can find out more about Adele by:
logging onto
www.adele.tv
or following her on Twitter
@OfficialAdele

Quote sources

Page 4 Myplay.com, 2009; **Page 6** *The Independent*, 2008; **Page 7** *Vogue Magazine*, 2012; **Page 8** *The Independent*, 2008; **Page 9** *The Sun*, 2012; **Page 11** *Entertainment Weekly*, 2008, www.adele.tv; **Page 13** www.adele.tv; **Page 15** *The Telegraph*, 2008 & 2011; **Page 17** www.adele.tv; **Page 19** *The Telegraph*, 2012; **Page 21** www.adele.tv; **Page 23** www.adele.tv; **Page 24** Billboard.com, *Vogue Magazine*, 2012; **Page 25** *The Independent*, 2008, *Vogue Magazine*, 2009, www.adele.tv; **Page 27** contactmusic.com, 2011;

You can read more about Adele in the following book:

Adele - The Biography by Chas Newkey-Burden (*Blake Publishing*, 2013)

GLOSSARY

7" vinyl single
A record disc pressed in vinyl and played on a turntable. There is usually one song on each side of the disc

A&R
Stands for artists and repertoire, the department of a record label that looks out for new talent

Billboard Hot 100
An American record chart that covers music of all types

CEO
Stands for chief executive officer, the top executive of a company

Empower
To give power

Feedback
Comments made by people on an event or piece of work

Genres
Different styles or categories

Haemorrhage
Bleeding from a broken blood vessel

HIV
Stands for human immunodeficiency virus. This virus can cause AIDS (stands for acquired immunodeficiency syndrome), an illness that weakens the immune system

Jazz
A type of music originally from black American culture in the early 20th century

Jazz hands
A flourish of the hands at the end of a song or dance

Joint venture
A business arrangement between two companies

Longevity
A long life

Lyrics
The words of a song

Masseuse
A person who gives massages

Myspace
A social networking site

Pioneering
Undertaking new ideas or ventures

R&B
Stands for rhythm and blues, a music genre

Venue
A place where something happens, usually a concert or sporting event

Index